BUGS
AND
BEASTIES

CHERYL NATHAN

COOL KIDS
P R E S S
Boca Raton, Florida

DEDICATED TO THE MEMORY OF MY FATHER

Copyright ©1995 by Cheryl Nathan

ISBN: 1-56790-516-1

First Printing

COOL KIDS PRESS
1098 N.W. Boca Raton Boulevard, Suite 1
Boca Raton, FL 33432

Printed in Singapore

Nathan, Cheryl, 1958-
    Bugs and beasties ABC / Cheryl Nathan.
        p. cm.
    ISBN 1-56790-516-1
    1. Animals--Juvenile literature. 2. English language--Alphabet-
-Juvenile literature. [1. Animals. 2. Alphabet.] I. Title.
    QL49.N315   1995
    591--dc20
    [E]   95-11534
                                                           CIP
                                                            AC

Aa

ant

Bb
butterfly

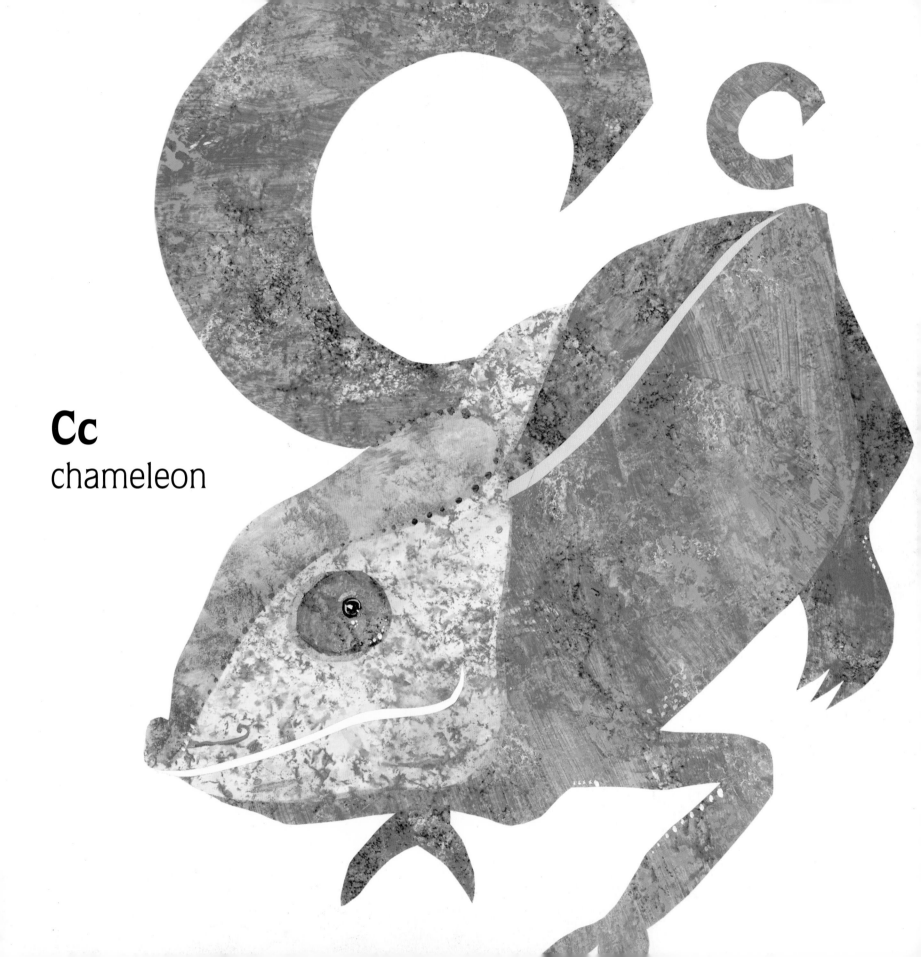

Cc
chameleon

Dd
dragonfly

Ee
echidna

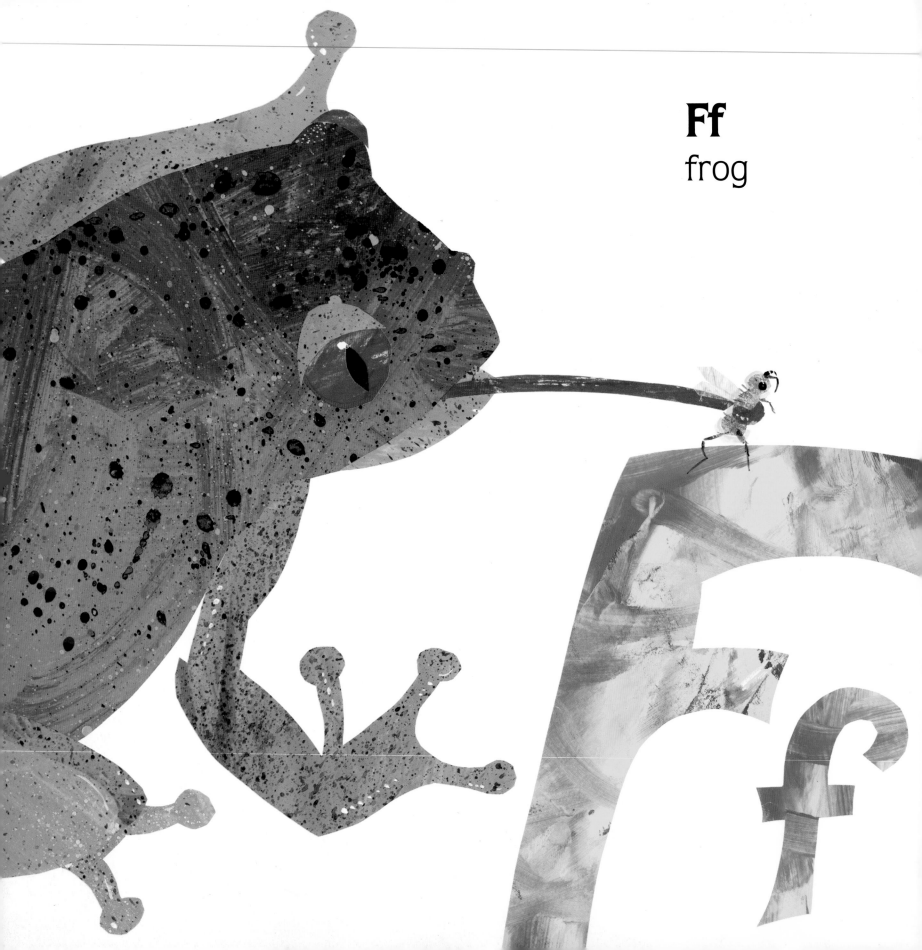

Ff
frog

Gg
grasshopper

Hh
hermit crab

Ii
iguana

Jj
jellyfish

Kk
kinkajou

Ll
lemur

Mm
millipede

Nn
newt

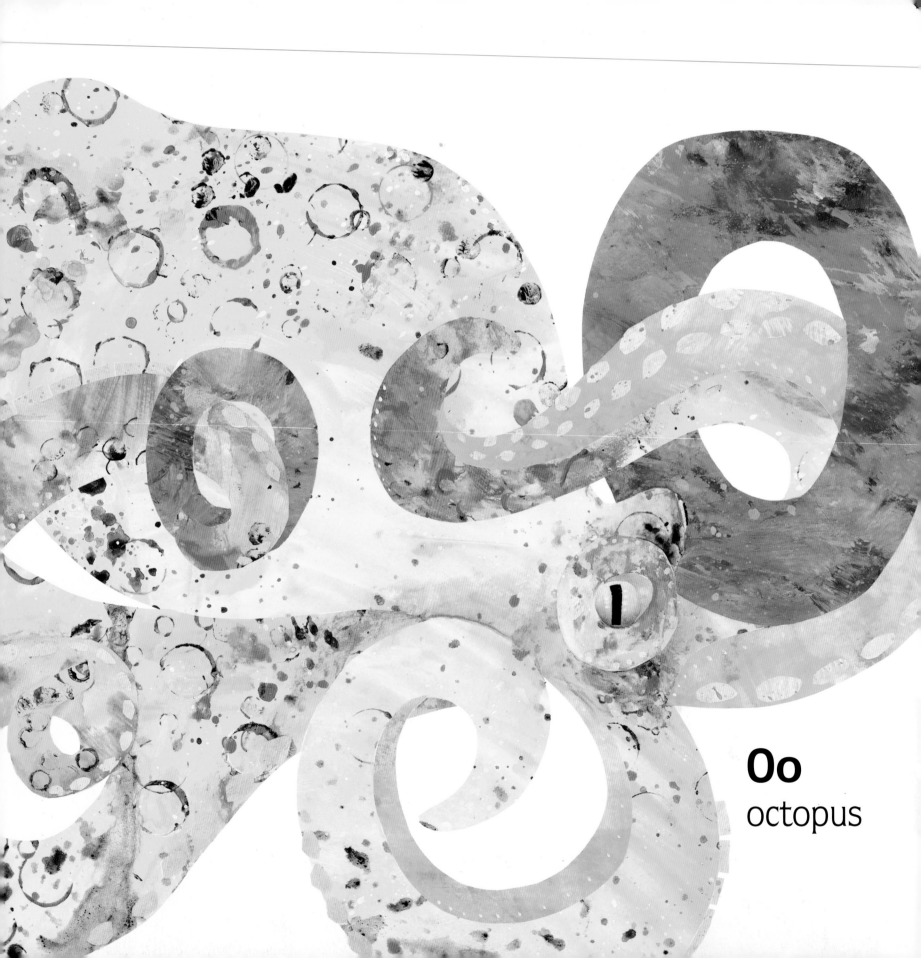

Oo
octopus

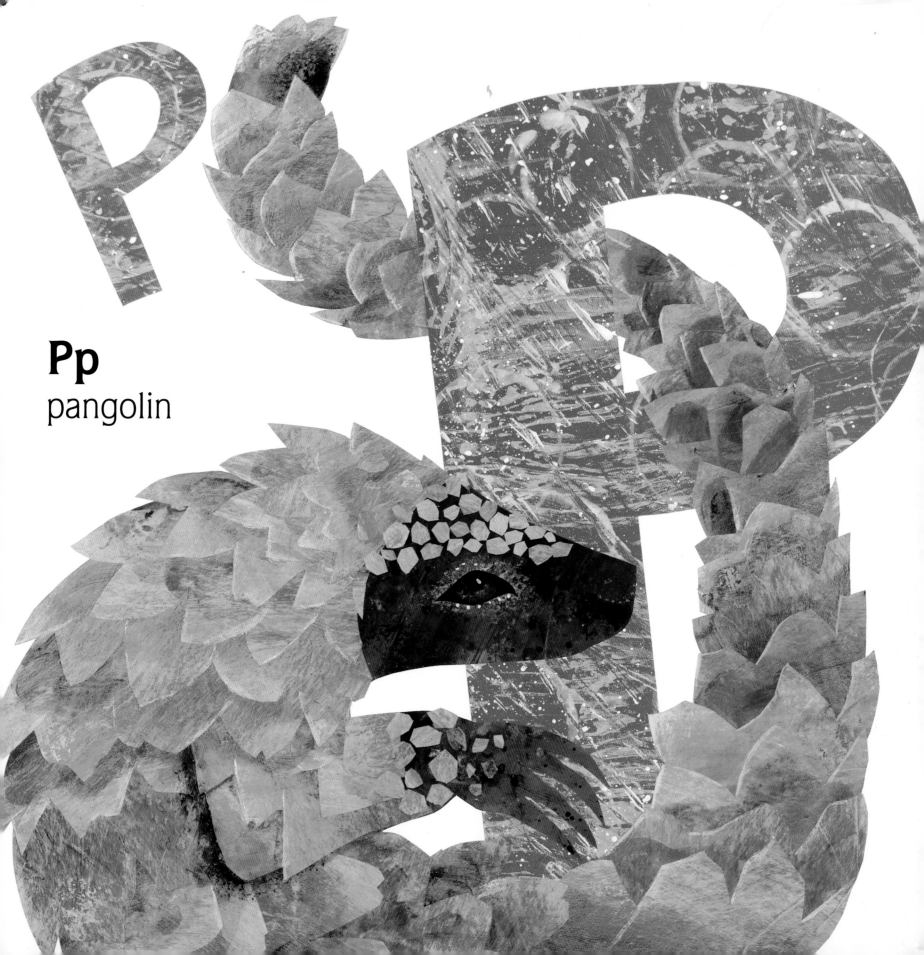

Pp
pangolin

Qq
quetzal

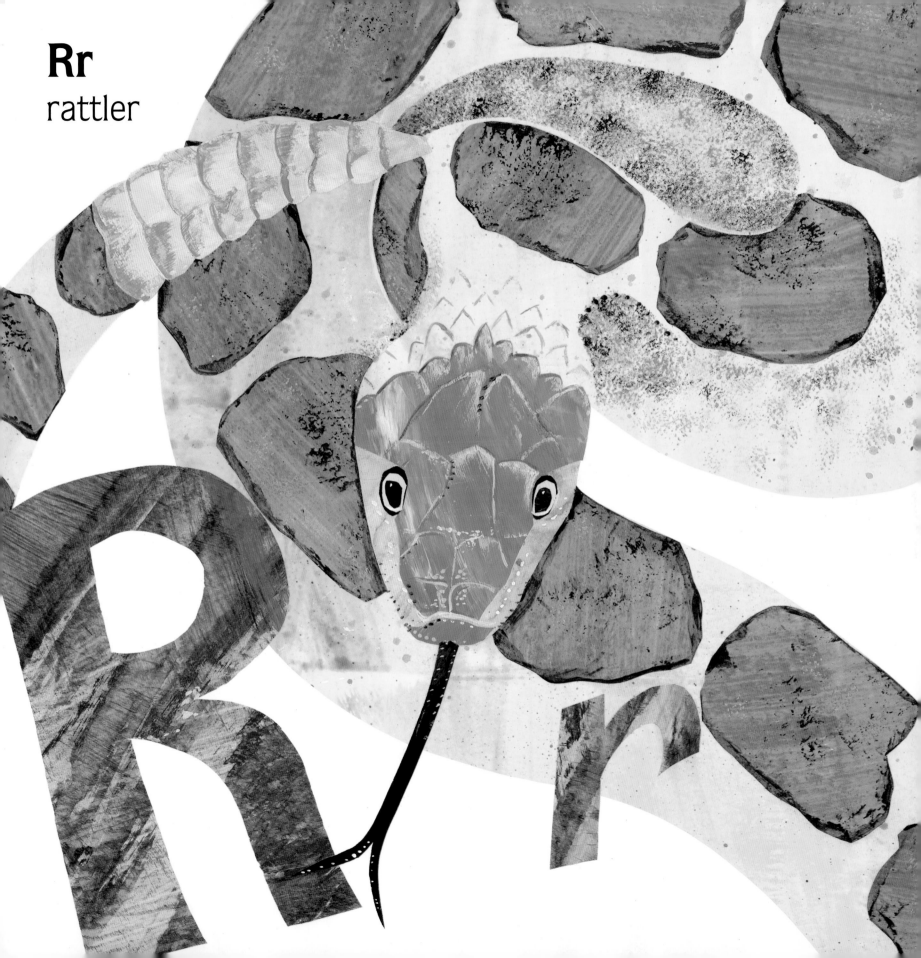

Rr
rattler

Ss
scorpion

Tt
tarantula

Uu
ursine howler

Vv
vampire bat

Ww
weevil

Xx Yy

extra-bright **y**ellow jacket

Zz
zorille

Ants live and work together in big communities. A tiny ant is so strong it can carry a load many times its own weight.

 Butterflies' wings are covered with thousands of tiny scales that give them their beautiful color. If you touch a butterfly's wing, the scales will come off. If they all came off, the wings would be perfectly clear. Butterflies are found all over the world.

 Chameleons can change their color from gray to brown to green, and sometimes even yellow! Changing their color helps chameleons hide from their enemies. Chameleons have very long sticky tongues that shoot out to catch flies and other insects.

 Dragonflies have two pairs of long, slender wings. When the front ones rise, the back ones fall. They live on ponds and fly very quickly and skillfully.

 Echidnas live all over Australia and are sometimes called spiny anteaters. They lay eggs with leathery shells and eat ants and termites. (Say "echidna" like this: i - **kid** - na.)

 Frogs live in water when they are babies, or tadpoles. But when they grow older most can breathe air and easily live on land. Frogs croak with their mouths closed.

 Grasshoppers are excellent jumpers. Some can cover 30 inches in a single leap! Grasshoppers have very good hearing too, but their ears are on their legs, not their heads.

 Hermit crabs wear their shells for protection. As their bodies grow, they have to keep leaving their shells to find new, bigger shells to wear. They are good climbers, and many people like to keep them as pets.

 Iguanas look like miniature dinosaurs, and some squirt a vapor from their nostrils like storybook dragons! They have strong claws and sharp teeth, but they rarely use them to fight.

 Jellyfish are found in almost every sea and ocean in the world. They are very beautiful to look at, but they sometimes sting swimmers who brush against them.

 Kinkajous live in trees in southern Mexico and the tropical forests of Central America. They use their long pink tongues to suck nectar out of flowers. (Say "kinkajou" like this: **king** - ka - joo.)

 Lemurs are gentle and curious members of the monkey family. They live in trees in Madagascar, and eat fruit and leaves. Some lemurs sleep during the day and stay awake all night. (Say "lemur" like this: **lee** - mur.)

Millipedes are born with just three pairs of legs. They continue to grow in length and grow more legs for two whole years. Some millipedes grow to eleven inches long, and some have stink glands they use to squirt a stinky fluid.

 Newts live in the water during the late spring and summer. Then in the autumn they go to dry land and burrow into the ground to sleep all winter. If a newt looses an arm or leg or tail, a new one will grow in its place.

 Octopuses live in oceans all over the world. Some are only two inches across when fully grown, and some grow to be 30 feet across and weigh 100 pounds. When frightened, octopuses can squirt out a cloud of black ink to hide behind.

 Pangolins use their 36-inch sticky tongues to sweep up ants and termites to eat. Their whole bodies are covered with hard scales. They live in Africa and tropical Asia. (Say "pangolin" like this: **pang** - guh - lin.)

 Quetzals live in the dense mountain forests of Central America, from southern Mexico to Costa Rica. They nest in holes in trees, and are recognized for their brightly colored feathers. (Say "quetzal" like this: ket - **sal**.)

 Rattlers, or rattlesnakes, are known for the warning signals they give by shaking the loosely-attached bony segments at their tails. They live in North America.

 Scorpions can go for many months without eating — even up to a year in some cases! They are feared for their powerful sting.

 Tarantulas are giant hairy spiders, and many people are afraid of them. Only a few kinds are poisonous though, and bites from most tarantulas are no more dangerous than a bee sting. They are actually easygoing creatures that only attack if they are threatened.

 Ursine howlers are monkeys that live in trees in northern South America. They use their strong tails to hang upside down from branches. Their howling is so loud it can be heard three miles away!

 Vampire bats live in Central and South America. During the day they sleep in dark caves. At night, they come out to feed on the blood of cattle and horses and other animals.

 Weevils have long, powerful snouts they use to drill into food. An acorn weevil uses her snout to drill into an acorn so she can lay her eggs inside the acorn for protection.

 Yellow jackets are protected by e**x**tra-bright coloring. Birds who eat insects are afraid of the yellow jacket's sting. The yellow jacket's bright yellow coat warns the birds to stay away.

 Zorilles look like skunks, but they are more closely related to weasels and polecats. Like skunks, they defend themselves by squirting a horrible-smelling liquid at their enemies. They are playful and make friendly, gentle pets. They live all over Africa. (Say "zorrille" like this: **zar** - ril.)